Made in United States
Troutdale, OR
02/24/2024

17917320R00070